PICTURE LIBRARY

VOLCANOES

PICTURE LIBRARY
VOLCANOES

Norman Barrett

Franklin Watts

London   New York   Sydney   Toronto

First Paperback Edition 1991

© 1989 Franklin Watts

First published in the USA by
Franklin Watts Inc
387 Park Avenue South
New York
NY 10016

ISBN 0-531-24618-3 (pbk.)
ISBN 0-531-10841-4 (lib.)
Number 89-5644

Printed in Italy

Designed by
Barrett and Weintroub

Photographs by
N.S. Barrett
Crater Lake National Park
Tony Eskrit
GeoScience Features
Hawaii Visitors Bureau/Greg Vaughn
NASA
Northern Ireland Tourist Board
David Oswin Expeditions
Pana-Vue
Malcolm A. Rose
Sólarfilma
Survival Anglia
USDA Forest Service/Jim Quiring

Illustration by
Rhoda and Robert Burns

Technical Consultant
Keith Lye

Contents

Introduction

Volcanoes are openings in the earth's surface through which eruptions of hot materials come from deep inside the earth. Most of these openings are on top of mountains, which are also called volcanoes.

The materials that are thrown out by volcanoes include hot gases, lava and pieces of rock. Lava is molten rock that usually comes out red hot.

△ Molten lava flows down the sides of a volcano like rivers of fire.

Many volcanic mountains are cone-shaped. They are formed around the openings by the material expelled during eruptions.

Volcanoes occur in many parts of the world – on continents, on islands and at the bottom of the sea. Some eruptions are so violent that they devastate large areas and cause great loss of life.

△ Dense clouds of ash, dust and gas pour forth from an island volcano.

Looking at volcanoes

Volcanic activity

Magma (molten rock) rises up from underground chambers. It may reach the surface through a vent (opening) of a volcano or a fissure (crack) in the ground. Geysers and hot springs may occur when underground water is heated by magma.

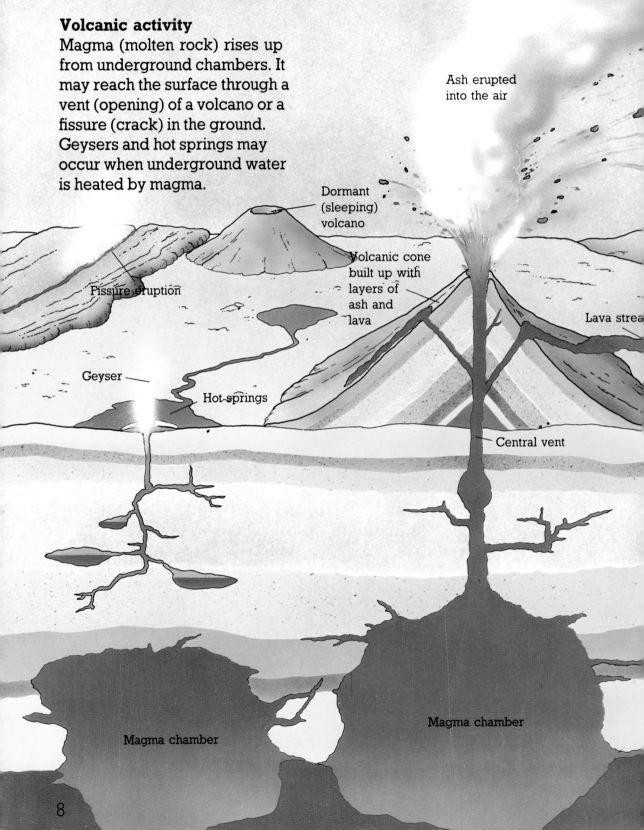

Ash erupted into the air

Dormant (sleeping) volcano

Volcanic cone built up with layers of ash and lava

Fissure eruption

Lava strea

Geyser

Hot springs

Central vent

Magma chamber

Magma chamber

Movements under the earth

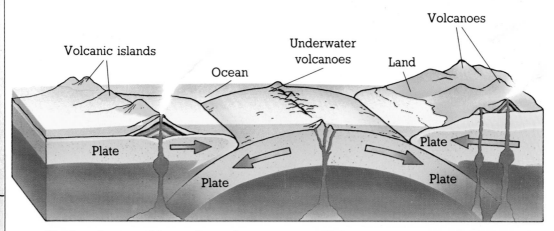

Volcanic islands

Ocean

Underwater volcanoes

Land

Volcanoes

Plate

Plate

Plate

Plate

Plate

Under the earth's surface, huge sections, called plates, of the earth's outer layers move slowly over molten rock. When plates collide or move apart, magma rises to the surface and erupts, forming volcanoes.

Volcanoes around the world

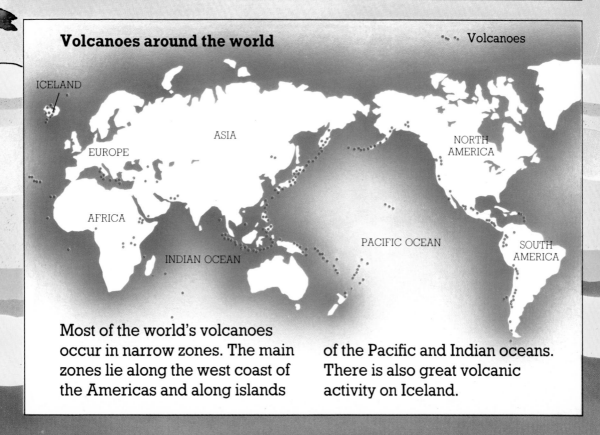

Volcanoes

ICELAND

ASIA

EUROPE

NORTH AMERICA

AFRICA

PACIFIC OCEAN

SOUTH AMERICA

INDIAN OCEAN

Most of the world's volcanoes occur in narrow zones. The main zones lie along the west coast of the Americas and along islands of the Pacific and Indian oceans. There is also great volcanic activity on Iceland.

Volcanic materials

Solids, liquids and gases all erupt from volcanoes. Lava is liquid. It flows down the sides of the volcano at speeds depending on how thick it is. It hardens into different formations as it cools.

Solid rock fragments exploded into the air are called tephra. They vary from tiny particles of dust to large pieces called "bombs."

The gas is mainly steam. When carrying volcanic dust, it looks like thick, black smoke.

△ Molten lava, volcanic "bombs" and ash are all present in this spectacular eruption in Iceland, home of many active volcanoes.

▷ Gas, dust and ash mix to form this dense cloud as the Indonesian volcano Krakatau erupts.

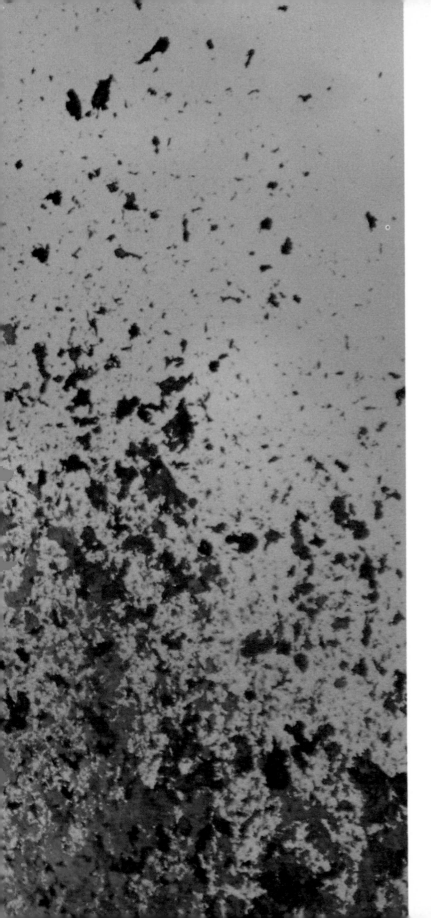

◁ A close-up of an eruption shows many different kinds of rock fragments being hurled into the air.

The tephra forms from magma that is so sticky, it traps any gas as it rises to the earth's surface. The pressure builds up so much that it blasts the magma into pieces.

The tiniest particles, the dust, are often carried vast distances in the earth's upper atmosphere.

Larger pieces, called ash, up to about 5 mm (0.2 in) across, fall back to earth and are welded together to form a rock called tuff.

The largest pieces, the volcanic "bombs," usually range between the size of a tennis ball and a football. But some measure more than a meter (3.3 ft) across and weigh as much as 100 tons.

Types of volcanoes

Volcanoes are classified in a number of ways. They may be classed as active, intermittent, dormant or extinct.

Active volcanoes are constantly erupting. Intermittent volcanoes erupt at regular intervals. Inactive volcanoes are either dormant ("sleeping") or extinct. Extinct volcanoes are ones that will probably never erupt again, but dormant volcanoes might.

△ An aerial view of Surtsey, an active volcano erupting. The volcano formed a new island off the south coast of Iceland in 1963, arising from eruptions on the ocean floor.

Another classification of volcanoes is based on their shape and how they were formed.

Cinder cones are formed when tephra erupts from a central vent and piles up around it.

Shield volcanoes build up when free-running lava spreads widely to form a low, dome-shaped mountain.

Strato-volcanoes form when lava and tephra from a central vent pile up in alternate layers to build up a cone-shaped mountain.

▽ The Spanish island of Tenerife, off the west coast of Africa, is dominated by Mount Teide. The highest point in the Atlantic Ocean, Teide is a dormant volcano. It is also a good example of a strato-volcano.

Types of eruptions

Volcanoes may also be classified according to the type of eruption.

The least violent are the Hawaiian eruptions, with fluid lava. In Strombolian eruptions, gas escaping from the magma produces tephra. The most violent eruptions occur when gas builds up tremendous pressure in sticky magma. This causes Vulcanian eruptions, with explosions of dust and "bombs," or Peléean eruptions, with explosions of clouds of hot ash and dust.

▷ The explosive eruption of Mt. St. Helens in 1980 is seen above the clouds. The top of the mountain was blasted clean off, devastating hundreds of square miles of Washington state.

▽ Rivulets of hot lava from a fissure eruption stream down the sides of Mt. Kilauea, in Hawaii.

◁ Fountains of fire dance on top of Mt. Etna, a volcano on the Italian island of Sicily.

This is a Strombolian type of eruption, named after Stromboli, an island volcano just north of Sicily in the Mediterranean Sea.

Volcanic effects

The immediate effects of volcanic eruptions can be devastating, with massive destruction and loss of human and animal life.

But volcanoes also bring benefits to mankind. Some of the rocks and minerals produced have uses, and volcanic ash becomes fertile soil. The energy produced in some volcanic regions is a valuable source of heat and power.

The less violent volcanoes provide spectacular tourist attractions.

▽ One of the many houses buried by lava during the eruption in 1973 on Heimaey, an island off the coast of Iceland. The people were evacuated, but the lava threatened to engulf the harbor. Sea-water was pumped into the lava flow for several weeks, slowing it down enough before the eruption stopped and the harbor was saved.

△ Runny lava cools on the surface and forms a smooth, folded rock called pahoehoe. This is sometimes called ropy, or corded, lava. Large areas of Hawaii and Iceland are covered with ropy lava. Some plants are able to grow on such terrain.

▷ The Giant's Causeway, a remarkable rock formation in Northern Ireland. It is made up of thousands of six-sided columns formed by an ancient lava flow.

△ Crater Lake, in Oregon, formed in the caldera of a volcano that erupted nearly 7,000 years ago. Wizard Island, near the rim of the crater, is a cone of cinders built up on a platform of lava.

▷ A chapel sits on top of a volcanic rock at Le Puy, in France. The plug of solid magma is all that is left of a volcano millions of years old.

◁ The Pinnacles, by Crater Lake, are towers of a volcanic rock called pumice.

Geysers and hot springs

Geysers and hot springs occur when water under the earth is heated by hot rock and spurts out at the surface.

Volcanic activity in some parts of the world is used to provide heat and electricity. This is called geothermal power, and is produced by underground steam. There are geothermal power stations in Hawaii, Iceland and New Zealand.

▽ Geothermal power is produced at the foot of a volcano in Iceland.

▷ Boiling mud and steam erupt from a geothermal area in Rotorua, New Zealand.

▽ Hot springs called Sulphur Cauldron, a colorful feature of Yellowstone National Park, in Wyoming. There are thousands of hot springs in this area as well as over 200 active geysers.

Volcanoes on other planets

Earth is not the only place where volcanoes occur. The Moon has many extinct volcanoes as well as lava flows billions of years old.

Huge volcanoes have been observed on Mars. Space probes sent to the outer planets have photographed erupting volcanoes on Io, a moon of the giant planet Jupiter.

△ Olympus Mons is a huge volcano on the planet Mars. It is three times the height of Mount Everest.

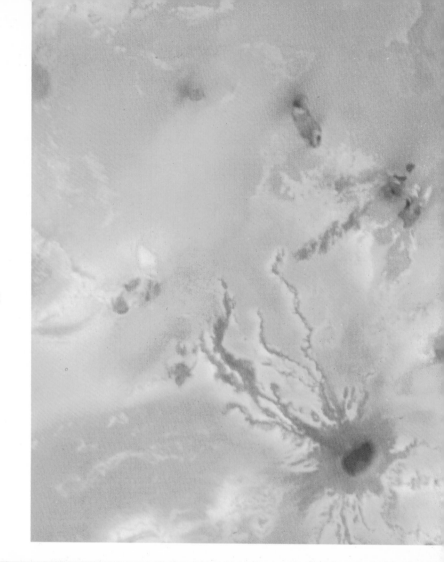

▷ A photograph of the surface of the moon Io taken by the Voyager space probe from about 125,000 km (77,000 miles). It shows what is thought to be a great lava flow from one of Io's active volcanoes (bottom right).

▽ A more distant shot of Io shows two blue volcanic eruption plumes about 110 km (70 miles) high.

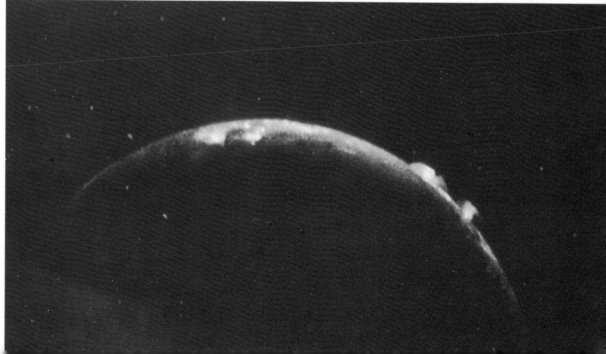

The story of volcanoes

△ Mount Vesuvius looms in the background as visitors explore the excavations at Pompeii. The town lay undiscovered for centuries after the eruption of Vesuvius in AD 79.

Moving plates

Scientists do not understand exactly why volcanoes occur. The most widely accepted theory is called plate tectonics.

Scientists believe that the earth's hard outer shell is split into large blocks called "plates." These move slowly over a layer of molten rock. When plates move apart, molten rock rises to fill the gap, sometimes forming volcanoes. When plates collide, one plate is often pushed beneath the other. Part of the plate forced down melts, and some of the molten rock is then forced to the surface through volcanoes.

The god of fire

Ancient peoples trembled at the sight and sounds of erupting volcanoes. They were regarded as signs from the gods. The ancient Roman god of fire was named Vulcan. The people believed he lived under an island off the coast. They called the island Vulcano.

The mighty Vesuvius

The best-known volcano of the ancient world was Vesuvius, in southern Italy. Its most explosive eruption occurred in AD 79, when Pompeii and other cities were buried under masses of hot ash.

Vesuvius is the only active volcano on the mainland of Europe. It has had many destructive eruptions in modern times, including three this century. Most eruptions since AD 79 have been accompanied by lava flows.

△ An artist's impression of an eruption of Vesuvius in 1872.

Studying volcanoes

The study of volcanoes is called volcanology. The people who study them are called volcanologists.

Observatories have been built on the slopes of many of the world's most dangerous volcanoes. The volcanologists

△ A volcanologist in protective clothing takes temperature measurements.

who work in these observatories use scientific instruments to record as much information about the volcanoes as possible. Volcanologists also study many of the world's other volcanoes.

Their instruments can detect the slightest earth tremor or bulging of the slopes, the release of any gases by the volcano and any temperature changes below the surface.

The records and observations made by volcanologists help them to detect volcanic activity and to predict future eruptions. It is not possible to stop an eruption, but people in the area can usually be evacuated in good time. In some cases it is possible to change the direction of the lava flow.

Mount St. Helens

There is still much to be learned about volcanoes. One volcano that has surprised the experts is Mount St. Helens, in Washington state. There were several minor eruptions in the mid-1800s, and more were predicted for the last few years of this century. But the ferocity of the 1980 explosion was a sharp reminder of the fiery furnaces that lie beneath the earth's crust.

△ A painting of Mount St. Helens by the Canadian artist Paul Kane shows an eruption of the 1840s being watched by local Flathead Indians.

Facts and records

△ The shattered Mount St. Helens, formerly a majestic cone-shaped mountain, stands in the background, while the logs of trees that were once a forest float on Spirit Lake or lie scattered over the bare landscape.

Death and destruction

In the 1980 Mount St. Helens eruption, the whole top of the mountain was blown off, leaving it 400 m (1,313 ft) shorter.

About 60 lives were lost, surprisingly few in view of the widespread destruction to plant and animal life.

The most disastrous eruption in recorded history was an explosion of Krakatau, an Indonesian island, in 1873. More than 35,000 people were killed by the sea wave it caused.

Old Faithful

Of the geysers in Yellowstone National Park, Old Faithful is the most famous, even though it is neither the world's largest nor the highest, nor is it the most consistent. But its height, the intervals between each spouting, and the time it spouts have changed little since it was first reported in 1870.

It spouts at intervals varying between ½ to 2 hours, sending cascades of hot water 30 to 55 m (100 to 180 ft) in the air. Each display lasts between 1½ and 5½ minutes, during which time as much as 50,000 litres (11,000 gallons) of nearly boiling water shoots into the air.

Steamboat Geyser, also in Yellowstone, has erupted to a height of 120 m (400 ft).

△ Old Faithful is a popular tourist attraction.

Glossary

Active
A volcano that is constantly erupting is said to be active.

Bomb
Volcanic bombs are large rock fragments that erupt from a volcano.

Caldera
A very large volcano crater.

Crater
The hole left around the vent of some volcanoes after an explosive eruption.

Crust
The earth's outer shell.

Dormant
An inactive volcano that has erupted in the past and can erupt again is said to be dormant.

Extinct
A volcano that is no longer active is said to be extinct.

Geyser
Hot water that erupts from the ground as a spout.

Intermittent
A volcano that erupts at regular intervals is said to be intermittent.

Lava
Molten rock flowing out of a volcano.

Magma
Molten rock below the earth's surface.

Pahoehoe
A smooth or ropy rock, formed by the cooling of runny lava.

Plate tectonics
The chief theory to explain volcanoes. It says that most volcanoes are caused by movements of vast sections of the earth's crust called plates.

Shield volcano
A low, dome-shaped volcano built up by free-running lava.

Strato-volcano
A cone-shaped volcano built up as lava and tephra form alternate layers.

Tephra
Any solid rock fragments that are hurled from a volcano.

Tuff
A rock formed from volcanic ash that has fallen back to earth.

Index